Total Quality Management
in a week

JOHN MACDONALD

Hodder & Stoughton

A MEMBER OF THE HODDER HEADLINE GROUP

Order queries: please contact Bookpoint Ltd, 130 Milton Park, Abingdon, Oxon OX14 4SB. Telephone: (44) 01235 827720, Fax: (44) 01235 400454. Lines are open from 9.00 - 6.00, Monday to Saturday, with a 24 hour message answering service. Email address: orders@bookpoint.co.uk

British Library Cataloguing in Publication Data
A catalogue record for this title is available from The British Library

ISBN 0 340 84946 0

First published 1993
Impression number 10 9 8 7 6 5 4 3 2 1
Year   2007 2006 2005 2004 2003

Cover image: Taxi/Getty Images
Typeset by SX Composing DTP, Rayleigh, Essex.
Printed in Great Britain for Hodder & Stoughton Educational, a division of Hodder Headline Plc, 338 Euston Road, London NW1 3BH by Cox & Wyman Ltd, Reading, Berkshire.

The leading organisation for professional management

As the champion of management, the Chartered Management Institute shapes and supports the managers of tomorrow. By sharing intelligent insights and setting standards in management development, the Institute helps to deliver results in a dynamic world.

Setting and raising standards

The Institute is a nationally accredited organisation, responsible for setting standards in management and recognising excellence through the award of professional qualifications.

Encouraging development, improving performance

The Institute has a vast range of development programmes, qualifications, information resources and career guidance to help managers and their organisations meet new challenges in a fast-changing environment.

Shaping opinion

With in-depth research and regular policy surveys of its 91,000 individual members and 520 corporate members, the Chartered Management Institute has a deep understanding of the key issues. Its view is informed, intelligent and respected.

For more information call 01536 204222 or visit www.managers.org.uk

■■■■■C O N T E N T S■■■■

The author can be contacted at:
19 Well House, Woodmansterne Lane, Banstead Village,
Surrey SM7 3AA   Tel: 01737 373552

The management of quality is accepted as a key issue for all organisations in both the private and public sectors. It involves everyone from the chief executive to the lowest paid worker. The Enron scandal and the demise of Arthur Andersen have led to a resurgence of TQM in the USA.

There are so many experts or 'gurus' on the subject of TQM that it can all seem very confusing. In reality it is the application of common sense rather than a complex academic subject.

The perceived need to be different or to be following the latest trend adds to the confusion. Titles such as *Continuous Improvement, Kaizan* or *Sigma Six* are essentially TQM in another guise.

The aim of this book is to 'clear the fog' and provide an easy step-by-step guide to the understanding of the TQM process.

We shall look at one step each day of the week.

The steps to understanding TQM

Sunday	– Understanding the principles
Monday	– Recognising the need to change
Tuesday	– Planning the change
Wednesday	– Changing the culture
Thursday	– Providing the tools and techniques
Friday	– Involving and helping the people
Saturday	– Ensuring success

What is TQM?

TQM stands for Total Quality Management.

Total means that everyone in the organisation is involved in the final product or service to the customer.

Quality does not just mean luxury. We need a way of describing quality that leaves no room for subjective opinion. The original definition was, 'quality means conformance to requirements'. That allows us to measure quality. We know when we do or do not conform to requirements. Everyone must understand quality in the same way. Once we are all speaking the same language of quality we can measure it and manage it.

Today's marketplace is now demanding that we go beyond this definition. The level of competition is steadily enhancing the customer's perception of what they consider is quality. A powerful definition of quality to meet these perceptions is 'quality means delighting the customer by continually meeting and improving upon agreed requirements'.

Management recognises that TQM will not happen by accident. TQM is a managed process which involves people, systems and supporting tools and techniques.

TQM is therefore a change agent which is aimed at providing a customer-driven organisation.

Why did TQM evolve?

For a long time customers accepted that things would go
wrong with their products. They were not pleased but
believed that it would be impossible to produce perfect
products or service. They tended to accept the salesman's
excuses or just shrugged their shoulders and said 'thats'
life'. The Japanese changed all that when they started to
produce products that did exactly what the salesman said
they would do. Every time and all the time. At first, their
Western customers were suspicious and then they came to
love Japanese products. Customers forgot about patriotism.
'British is Best' or 'America First' were great slogans but the
customers ignored the slogans when they were spending
their hard-earned money. All of a sudden, quality became a
matter of economic survival. Motorbikes, cycles, cars, TV
sets, videos and cameras: all were invented in the West but
now the Western customers were buying them from Japan.

The result? Customer power now reigns supreme. The old
common law principle 'let the buyer beware' has become
'let the seller beware'. The customer is now supported by
consumer organisations and governments now legislate in
favour of the consumer.

What's special about the Japanese?
Nothing. Forty years ago the Japanese were famous for
selling tawdry rubbish and cheap imitations of Western
goods. So it was not the five-thousand-year-old Japanese
culture that was responsible for the quality of their
products. As late as the 1950s they decided to change the
plan. Their new aim was to achieve world economic
dominance with quality products.

First they travelled and studied how Western industry achieved quality. They listened to American quality experts like Drs Juran and Deming who could not get a hearing in the West. They were surprised at what they found and believed that they could do better. At that time, the West believed that quality came from increasing the level of inspection; that is, finding all the bad components that had been made before they reached the customer. It was a very expensive exercise as we shall see.

Cost of quality

Inspection based quality meant that higher quality was achieved by increasing the level of inspection. The result was a mounting level of rejects or a reworking of defective products. Management thus viewed quality as an expensive addition to operating costs. In the prevailing extreme of short-term financial management, quality became a matter of compromise. Management tried to find an optimum level of quality, one that would satisfy or partially satisfy *most* of their customers. At that stage, customers did not have a choice. Managers did not have to change their viewpoint because all business worked that way.

Then the customer did have a choice. The Japanese had learnt to work another way. They invested in prevention, which means *make it right first time*. Quality was no longer an expensive addition. In the words of American quality guru Philip Crosby, 'quality is free'. If you do not make any bad components, you do not need all this expensive inspection, rejection and rework.

Crosby was able to demonstrate to executives that the cost of their traditional practices amounted to some 25% of sales revenue. For every four components they produced they might as well have thrown one away. In the service sector costs were shown to be nearly 50% of operating costs. The Japanese in studying the West had learnt that lesson twenty years before. A simple concept that was to turn the business world upside down.

Fortress management
Managers are not stupid. They know that quality is important. They want better communication, participation and teamwork. However, traditional management practices make it difficult.

Organisations manage people and work through functional departments. The manager and people within these departments are dedicated to their *own* objectives. They work hard as a team. Unfortunately, their objectives are usually divisive. Each department is competing, rather than collaborating, with each other. The traditional system has created 'departmental fortresses', creating barriers to communication across the organisation.

Achieving 'zero defects'
Most quality initiatives are based on the elimination of
error, or 'zero defects'. This may appear an incredible step
forward and would certainly represent a major cost benefit.
However, it is not enough to achieve world-class quality
status. It is also necessary to reduce variation and stimulate
innovation.

Reducing variation
Management recognise tolerances in the output of work
processes. These tolerances are accepted to account for
variation. There is variation in everything: tools wear out,
materials are never exactly the same, variation in one area
can effect the time to complete in another area.
Management rarely measure these variations. So how do
they know that the tolerances are right or the best that can
be achieved? TQM provides tools, such as statistical process
control (SPC), which enable us to measure and thus reduce
variation.

Innovation
Releasing the potential of people to think about their work
will stimulate innovation. The car manufacturer Toyota
claims to get more than one million ideas a year from their
people. The Japanese have not invented one element in the
process of photography, but to the customer the modern
Japanese camera appears to be a new invention and they
now dominate that market. This is because thousands of
little innovations have steadily improved the camera. That
is the power of innovation. Understanding of the power of
innovation has spurred the emergence of the
complementary concept of TQM called Knowledge
Management.

The principles of TQM

The process chain

One of the basic elements of TQM is the 'process chain'. Work is not isolated within the 'departmental fortresses', it is divided into a series of activities or processes. Each work process links with another process and the work output of one process forms the input for another. In fact every organisation operates through a chain of interlinked processes, which work through and across departmental boundaries.

The strength of the total chain to the ultimate customer is reliant on the weakest link; an individual process. Failure in any one process will have an impact on the final product or service. The secret of quality is to ensure that each link is equally strong; 'getting it right first time' at each stage.

Every organisation has hundreds of either manufacturing or administrative work processes. People may work alone or with others at each stage. Operating a machine on a factory floor, typing a letter, preparing an insurance policy, admitting a patient to a hospital or receiving a guest at a hotel are all work processes. All are different but they all have something in common. Each of those processes has a customer and a supplier. We can call them our **internal** customers and suppliers.

Internal customers and suppliers
In most processes, the customers are not the final customers of the organisation; they are **internal customers**. In our examples the hospital administrator and the hotel receptionist do have contact with the external customer, but their work processes also have internal customers. If their work is completed right first time it will enable the ward sister to greet the patient, or the housekeeper to have the room ready for the guest, on time.

A fundamental objective of TQM is to ensure that everyone realises that they are in a customer-supplier relationship. The customer they have to delight is the customer of *their* process. If the chain remains intact, the ultimate customer will also be delighted. To do this we have to *know* what our customer wants. We have to learn to communicate with our colleagues so that we fully understand their requirements. Many of these colleagues will be outside our own cosy fortress.

Few of the problems we meet at work are technical and it is also rare to meet totally new problems. Usually, the same old problem crops up time and time again. Understanding the nature of the work processes will help remove many repetitive errors. The majority of day-to-day hassles are caused by a failure in communication, the behaviour of management, or the attitude of people.

Communication
Modern executives are keenly aware of the importance of communication. Team briefings, in-house magazines, notice boards and videos featuring the chief executive are common. Unfortunately, these are rarely about real work situations and are usually misdirected.

Communication is usually directed downwards from the top. It has the laudable objective of keeping the workers informed. But there are few opportunities for the workers to keep the managers informed. Yet the people doing the job are more likely to know about work problems than the managers. Workers need their own opportunity to set the agenda for communication.

TQM is about changing the traditional communication culture by changing the behaviour of management. The two key changes in behaviour that are needed are:

- learning to listen
- empowering employees to set the agenda for communication

Bring joy to work
Management is obsessed with the numerate measurement of people. It sets objectives which create anxiety or fear in the organisation. People alone are relatively powerless to influence the overall result, for most of the problems met are caused by the system not the people. Management should concentrate on measuring the system, the chain of processes, rather than measuring people. Ensure that the system works and set objectives for people that create trust and collaboration. Bring joy to work.

In summary, these are the reasons for implementing TQM:

- Increasing competitive pressure
- The changing perceptions of the customer
- The hidden waste under the present methods
- To change the perceptions of managers and people
- To release the potential of people
- Survival

The benefits of TQM

These are so enormous that they sound like a confidence trick. They represent the impossible business dream; a total win/win situation!

The benefits of TQM can be summarised as:

- A greatly improved product or service
- A major decrease in wasted resources
- A massive leap in productivity
- The best opportunity to increase profit
- A long-term increase in market share
- A sustained competitive advantage
- A real release of the potential of people
- A motivated workforce
- The elimination of much hassle and frustration involved in management

The claims are so great that it would be folly to ignore them. Ask yourself the question, 'How did the Japaneses perform their miracle?'. Remember that they have no natural resources and are thousands of miles from their markets. Remember that less than fifty years ago their products were a shoddy mimicry of Western goods.

Barriers to TQM

We can see that the principles of TQM are really the application of common sense. However, inertia and the power of tradition are not easy obstacles to overcome. Research shows that a substantial proportion of companies who launch TQM initiatives are disappointed. They all improved but they did not meet their original expectations.

The reasons for disappointment with TQM can be summarised as:

- A lack of management commitment
- A lack of vision and planning
- A satisfaction with the quick fix
- The process of change became tool-bound
- The culture change and project approach conflicted
- Quality management became bureaucratic
- Management did not change its behaviour
- The people were not really involved
- A lack of business measurables to measure TQM

Over the next six days we shall examine a way to overcome these barriers. We start on Monday by understanding how to assess the need to change in our own organisation.

Summary

To sum up, TQM:

- Is a change agent
- Aims to provide a customer-driven organisation
- Provides new management methods
- Removes departmental fortresses
- Recognises process chains
- Changes management behaviour
- Changes employees attitudes
- Releases innovative potential

Assessing the need

On Sunday we looked at the principles of TQM. We saw that TQM was essentially a change agent to take us from our present culture to a new management culture. A culture based on the customer and continuous improvement.

Today, we may have a successful company, using our tried and tested management methods. However, we should assess whether we need to change, and discover if there is an opportunity to improve. Even if we already recognise the need, we need information on our present status to help us plan the journey to continuous improvement.

We should base our assessment of the current culture on:

- Our competitive position
- How our customers and suppliers see us
- How our managers and people see us
- How well we communicate with each other
- How well we work in teams
- How we view quality
- The cost of hidden waste
- Our company objectives; do they create collaboration and trust between us?
- Our key priorities for improvement

Finding the answers

Answering all those questions may seem a formidable task. Indeed it would be a major job if we had to carry out a full competitive analysis, a full employee survey and an accurate assessment of the cost of waste. However, for our purpose, we do not need to go to that level of detail. At this stage we are assessing our perception of these issues and of the need to change. If management perceive no reason to change; nothing will happen.

Perceptions
We all have perceptions about how our own organisation works and we may find that our perceptions differ from those of colleagues in other departments or at other levels. Our opinions have been built up by our day-to-day experiences. In time, we all tend to make decisions or to behave to one another on the basis of our individual perceptions. In this way our perceptions become self-prophesising elements that make up the culture of our organisation.

Questioning
Assessment is about questioning, so we are going to spend most of Monday asking questions about our perceptions. To begin with, we need to assess our view of the organisation on its:

- present state
- communication in the workplace
- use of teamwork
- level of hidden waste.

As a result, we will be in a better position to seek the answer to further questions and decide whether there is a need to change.

Start by completing the questionnaire on the next page.

The present state of the organisation

If we were able to complete the questionnaire with every tick in the 'excellent' column we have also completed the assessment. We are unlikely to need TQM and we can close the book now.

Assessment 1

Please show your rating for each question by ticking one of the boxes. Tick one box only for each question.

	POOR	MODERATE	AVERAGE	GOOD	EXCELLENT
1 How I rate our services versus the competition	We are struggling – sell by price alone	Not too bad – we have some good features	Reasonable standard – no serious problems	Up to industry standards	Best in the industry – always delight the customer
2 How I believe our customers see us	Customer complaints are a serious problem	We usually sort out customer problems	Not too many complaints	They keep coming back – must like us	We keep in close contact – delighted with us
3 How I believe our suppliers see us	Never know that they want – bad payers	Do not always know what they want – otherwise OK	No problem but always price dominated	Usually know what they want – easy to work with	Absolutely clear requirements – a real partnership
4 How I believe employees see the organisation	Never know where they are – can't make up their minds	Not too bad as employers go	Always fair – no complaints	A good company	Proud to be with us
5 How I believe the competition see us	Forgotten they where still in the market	Pick up some of their dissatisfied customers	Pretty good – we win some, we lose some	Tough competitors	Out of our league

But most of us will need to carry on questioning. There are a number of possible reasons why we fall short of the very best. A common reason is the lack of a declared purpose for the organisation and a vision for its future. Check whether that applies in your company by answering the following questions:

1 Do we have a mission, or purpose, statement?
2 Do we have supporting principles and values which define how we are going to operate?
3 Does everyone of us in the company know what they are?
4 Do we all know how we are to change our behaviour because of them?

If any of those questions received a 'No' answer we have some input to our planning session on Tuesday. Our assessment questionnaires used today concentrate on our internal perceptions, but of course we also need to assess the perceptions of our customers, suppliers and others. The author uses up to fifteen different questionnaires in helping companies to meet Tuesday's planning requirements. The growing need to measure the perceptions of customers has spawned a major new field for consultants. The complementary need to understand the practices and processes of competitors and other companies has led to the concept of Benchmarking.

We should now proceed to complete assessment questionnaires 2 and 3.

Assessment 2
(teamwork)

Please show your rating for each question by ticking one of the boxes. Tick one box only for each question.

	1 (low)	2	3	4	5 (high)
1 How well do individuals managers work together?					
2 How well do departments work together?					
3 How do you rate communication in the organisation?					
4 How do you rate your communication with subordinates?					
5 How do you rate your subordinates' communication with you?					

Assessment 3
(attitudes)

Please show your rating for each question by ticking one of the boxes. Tick one box only for each question.

	1 (low)	2	3	4	5 (high)
1 How serious are you about quality?					
2 How serious is management about quality?					
3 How serious are employees about quality?					
4 How good is employee morale?					
5 How do you rate the organisation on management education?					
6 How do you rate the organisation on employee communication?					

Communication

In assessment questionnaire 2 we rated our perceptions on a number of communication issues, one of which related to our communication with our boss. The following questions test that perception further:

- Do I believe that my boss wants to know about my work problems and help me solve them?
- Do I tell my boss about my problems?
- Do I know exactly what is required of me?
- Do I sometimes just muddle through?
- Do I always get my work right first time?
- Would my boss understand my problems?

The answers to these questions should give us an insight into how well the organisational culture supports good communication about work.

Strength of process chains

All work is a process. We work in one or many, often small, processes which go together to complete the service chain to our external customers. Typical processes are typing a letter, completing a report, machining a component, completing an airline ticket, or scheduling a hospital operating theatre. We can test the strength of our chain of processes by selecting one we work in and asking the following questions:

- What is the output of the process?
- Who are the customers (internal or external) who receive this output?
- Have we agreed the requirements for that output with our customer?
- Are we absolutely clear about those requirements?
- What inputs do we need?
- Who is the supplier of those inputs?
- Have we agreed the requirements we need for input with our supplier?

If we are unclear or negative about the answer to any of these questions, we are likely to encounter delay, confusion or will have to redo the work! Each of those results contributes to hidden waste.

Cost of waste

Waste on a factory floor is obvious and so plant managers concentrate on keeping it to a minimum, but most organisations also have a massive level of hidden waste of resources. Because it is hidden in day-to-day operations, little effort is made to reduce this costly waste. In manufacturing the total waste typically amounts to 25% of sales revenue. It is not unusual to find waste levels in service industries which cost 40% to 50% of operating costs. TQM can help us identify and then reduce or eliminate these costs.

Nonconformances

On Sunday we described quality as 'conformance to requirements'. Each time we fail to meet a requirement first time we have a nonconformance. Waste is the accumulative cost of these nonconformances throughout the organisation.

Typical nonconformances of varying functions are:

- warranty expense
- staff turnover
- equipment failure
- excess inventory
- overdue accounts receivable
- inspection to find errors in work
- corrective action
- scrap
- computer downtime
- invoicing errors
- unplanned maintenance
- cost of injuries
- direct debit errors
- customer complaints
- rework
- bad debt
- incorrect forecasts
- lost documents

A useful indication of the level of waste in our organisation is to make a quick assessment of how we use our time in our own function. Try answering the following questions:

What percentage of weekly time is spent in our operation on:

- Troubleshooting or solving problems?
- Chasing other departments for work or information?
- Redoing work?
- Providing information we have provided before?
- Dealing with customer complaints?
- Attempting to find out what is really required?
- Doing unscheduled tasks?

Add up all those percentages to give a rough estimate of the weekly time spent as a result of nonconformances in our operation. Note that many of these nonconformances are caused outside our own department.

Our assessment

So far today we have been assessing our own perceptions and getting a rough idea of the cost of waste in our own operation. This may have given us a personal ownership of the need for improvement. However, we do not work alone and, as we have seen, many of our problems are caused by bad communication or events outside our control. Therefore, improvement will need the collaboration of our colleagues and they are unlikely to change unless they also recognise the need.

Overall assessment

We can help the overall assessment and recognition of need by introducing our colleagues to the same questioning we have undertaken. Tomorrow, we will see how to achieve this teamwork.

Agenda for organisation assessment

1 Bring together the heads of all departments for a presentation on TQM (another book in this series, *Successful Presentation*, will help you.)

2 Following your presentation, ask each attendee to complete similar questionnaires to those you have completed. Remember that the spread of perceptions is an indicator to the level of shared purpose and values of the organisation.

3 Ask each of them over the next few days to discuss with their subordinates the possibility of nonconformances and waste in their operations. Make certain that they understand that these nonconformances are often caused by events outside their control; this will make

them less defensive about their own departments. They do not need to cost their answers.

4 The following week, arrange for each to be interviewed to collect the data. Similar questions to those you have answered can be used to facilitate these interviews.

5 Invite the finance department to cost the results of the interviews.

6 Assemble all the data in presentation form. Reconvene the group and present the findings.

Review of findings

The presentation of the findings of the overall assessment is likely to provoke discussion which should be encouraged. The results of such discussions would usually include:

- A divergence of individual perceptions of the standing of the organisation from the viewpoint of customers, suppliers and employees.
- A general recognition of the barriers to communication caused by 'departmental fortresses'.
- A surprised recognition of the level of unnecessary waste in the organisation. (Note: typically only half the level of real waste is found at this juncture but most will recognise that more exists.)
- Identification of some key areas for improvement.

Recognition and acceptance of need

A general reaction to this kind of assessment is, 'What are we going to do about it?'. In other words, there is a recognition and acceptance of the need to change. On Tuesday we will answer this basic question.

Summary

We have spent Monday questioning the need for change in our organisation. What did our assessment show us about our organisation and its:

- Present status and culture?
- Communication and teamwork?
- Vision and values?
- Attitude to people?
- Level of waste?
- Need to change?

In every company or public service organisation that the author has worked with, the answers to these questions have convinced the executives, managers and other employees that there is a real need to change. Even more interesting this has been true of countries as diverse as the USA, India, Eastern Europe, Mexico and the UK.

Planning for success

Yesterday our assessment demonstrated the need for improvement in our work processes and for a change in our management culture. We saw that to be a world-class quality organisation we need a business strategy based on continuous improvement.

On Sunday, we recognised that TQM was the change agent best suited to achieving the new culture. But we still have to answer the question, '*How* would we use TQM in our organisation?'.

Today we start answering that question by preparing a plan for the implementation of a TQM process in our **unique** situation.

Establishing a planning team

In a small organisation (under 250 employees) the planning team should be the senior management team. In a larger group the executives are likely to appoint **facilitators** to prepare a detailed plan for their approval. The facilitators will also drive the initial implementation.

There are some essential rules to follow in selecting a team of facilitators.

Composition of planning team

1 Senior and respected managers who represent:
 • all major functions within the organisation
 • all major operational locations
2 Within these parameters the team should include:
 • women and minority groups
 • sceptics or strong neutrals who will question the process

It is advisable to use an experienced TQM consultant to facilitate the development of a plan. With their help the selected team will need a minimum of four days to develop the outline plan. The final plan will require additional 'working-up time'.

A business plan for quality

Experience has shown that, all too often, managers do not plan for, and manage quality as they manage their other key projects. Once the need for change has been recognised there is a tendency to rush out to enthuse the organisation with the need for quality. In many companies this has resulted in a short-term programme or motivational exercise, cynically referred to as the 'flavour of the month'.

We do not intend to make that mistake. When we contemplate other key projects or changes to operations we prepare a business plan. We are going to do the same for quality. After all, this is probably the largest project that we have ever tackled in the organisation. It is almost certainly the first project that has involved every employee. We also intend to maintain the impetus for quality improvement year after year. Our 'Business Plan for Quality' is therefore the first step for the inclusion of quality in all subsequent operational business plans.

What do we want in our plan?
Before we start the planning process, we should have a clear idea about our objectives and what we want to include in the plan. Remember that this is a plan for *our* organisation only.

Consider what was learnt about TQM on Sunday, and the results of the assessment conducted on Monday, then answer the following questions:

1 What is the intended objective or outcome?
2 Is this a strategic or tactical plan?
3 What are our principal concerns about implementing TQM?
4 What were the major problems identified in the assessment?
5 How are we going to convince everyone in the organisation of the need to change?
6 Who is going to manage quality?
7 How will we know that TQM is working?
8 Should this be a 'top down' or 'bottom up' plan?

Refer to your answers as we proceed with the plan.

Objectives of the plan

The key impediments to the success of TQM are the lack of:

- a vision and direction for the organisation
- management comprehension of what has to happen and their role in the process
- real business measurables and goals for success

Our plan must therefore provide:

- specific management direction and goals for results
- detailed implementation activities to support systematic organisational change
- details of the resources required

Components of the plan

To meet out plan objectives we will need to define the following plan components:

- Vision, principles and values for the organisation
- Management structure for change
- Education and training for every employee
- Systems and tools needed to support the process
- Key opportunities and priorities for improvement
- Implementation tactics
- Goals and criteria for success
- Resources required

For the rest of today we will examine each of these components in turn.

Vision, principles and values

Before looking at this component of the plan, we need to ask whether the organisation has:

- a clear purpose statement, or vision of what it is and where it is going
- a set of principles and values which define its relationships with its customers, suppliers and employees

Now we need to ask whether every employee knows:

- the vision or where the organisation wants to go?
- the principles and values of the organisation, or how their behaviour is supposed to change to accomplish the organisation's objectives?

If your answer to all these questions is a resounding yes, this component of the plan is fundamentally completed. However, it might still be helpful to re-examine these statements and reconsider them in the light of our new knowledge. In any case they will bear repeating and including in the plan.

If the answer is no to any of the questions, we clearly have some work to do. We are planning to develop or change our culture to achieve continuous improvement. Unless we can define that objective in the terms of our organisation it is a pointless exercise.

Sharing the vision
We learnt from the principles of TQM that we could not expect to release the potential of employees unless they could share the vision and purpose of the organisation. The leaders must therefore have a vision to share. The plan must define that vision or, if it does not exist, it must be developed.

It is vital that the chief executive and key colleagues agree the purpose and vision before it is announced to the organisation as a whole. If these senior executives are part of the planning team there is no problem but they often delegate planning to a lower level. In that case a separate meeting should be arranged to finalise this key message.

No outsider can define your vision but there are some guidelines which could be helpful. First the negative traps which are so easy to fall into. For example, the purpose of:

- an airline is not to fly airplanes but to transport people by air
- hospital administrators is not to manage hospitals but to provide successful healthcare
- manufacturing companies is not to produce perfect products but to satisfy a consumer need in a specific area

There are profound differences in those purposes which go to the heart of the quality revolution. Turning to the positive, it is possible to define some guidelines which every combination of vision and supporting principles and values should include. These are as follows:

- successful visions or purpose statements are always customer orientated
- for future success they should define wider responsibilities to the community in which the organisations operate
- the supporting principles and values should define the organisation's responsibilities and intended behaviour towards their customers, suppliers and employees
- they should also define the behavioural culture between management and employees, and between employees themselves

- a definition of success, profit and business
  measurables are part of the vision and values
- they are not pious statements but must always be
  relevant to the organisation and its people

Finally they must be lived: in too many companies the
Chairman's video about the value of the company are
greeted by employees with cynical comments such as, 'I
wish I worked for that company'.

Sharing a common language

As we move through the week we shall be developing the
common language for communicating objectively about
quality and our work processes. What is important is that
everyone should know what they mean when they use the
word quality. We must therefore start by selecting or

developing a definition for quality that is suitable for our organisation. This definition should be included in the plan.

In developing a definition for quality we must avoid subjective words such as excellence or goodness. These words mean something different to everyone and provide no basis for measuring whether we have achieved quality.

Commonly used definitions of quality

- Fitness for purpose
- Conformance to requirements
- Delighting the customer by continuously meeting, and improving upon, agreed requirements

Management structure for change

We do not need to develop a separate structure to manage quality. Indeed to do so would defeat the purpose and create another departmental fortress. Managers and people working together in normal structure will be responsible for managing quality.

However, in the early stages of the TQM process we will need a shadow organisation to plan and implement change. An example of such an organisation is illustrated in the diagram below. Our plan must include a similar diagram designed to match our own management organisation.

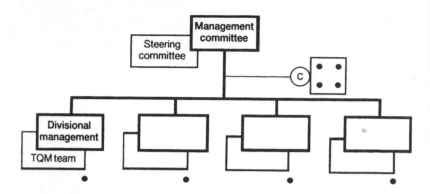

The steering committee and the TQM teams are effectively the management committee and the divisional or departmental management teams meeting separately to focus on the process of change. The black dots represent facilitators and other specialists to provide support for the process. A central co-ordinator for quality (a member of the management committee) may also from time to time chair a meeting of facilitators. The responsibility of the steering committee and the TQM teams is to plan and design the systems and tools to be used in the process. These teams are never responsible for managing quality and therefore the shadow organisation will only remain in place *during the initial phases*.

Education and training

On the first two days of the week, we came to the conclusion that we wanted to create a culture based on continuous improvement. A culture that could be shared by everyone. This shared culture will not be achieved overnight; it will take time. So far today we have worked on developing the values of the new culture. Later in the week we will spend time on the knowledge required to change to continuous improvement.

The most powerful vehicle available to us to achieve that change is education and training. There is a difference between these two elements. For example, we may agree that our children need sex education but there would not be the same measure of agreement that they also need practical sex training. In business we want to influence people's attitudes so that they take common ownership of the need to change and also learn the skills of using communication and problem-solving tools. Some selected people will also need to know how to manage change.

Education and training is therefore the fulcrum in implementing the TQM process. Clearly we need to include a detailed schedule for education in our plan. When considering this issue, the following questions should be asked:

1 Will everyone in the organisation require the same education?
2 Does every employee have the same role in the TQM process?
3 If you decide that the executives, managers, specialists and workers have different roles, how would you divide their educational needs?
4 Is education at work the same as education at school?
5 What is the most persuasive element of adult education?
6 What are the advantages and disadvantages of a single two to three-day course and 10 weekly sessions of two hours each? (Consider this from the perspectives of educational value and scheduling.)
7 Would the standard TQM courses available in the market achieve change in our organisation?
8 Would external or internal trainers be most effective in achieving change in our organisation?

Adult learning in business is most effective when it directly relates to the workplace. Employees at all levels are more likely to understand and retain knowledge if they have an easy transition with practice of the new concept and then an immediate opportunity to apply the concept to their own work.

Traditional TQM courses have a tendency to create indigestion with the number of concepts. They will include case history workshops but rarely provide the opportunity to prove the theory in live action. The most effective method for the student is to break down the concepts into small bites, which can be practised with colleagues in a workshop and then immediately tested in their own environment. Situations will vary but generally 10 two-hour sessions at weekly intervals are more powerful than 20 hours of solid course learning.

Experience has also proved that in-house instructors (preferably managers rather than from the training department) are more effective than external specialists. The standard package, though tempting, is more likely to create communication barriers than remove them.

We will return to the material content and the needs of differing employee roles on Thursday. Our plan will need to include a schedule for employee education and training defining the time to complete, the number of in-house instructors and the resource commitment.

Systems and tools

Many systems and tools have been developed to support the TQM process. A few are sophisticated statistical processes demanding specialised knowledge. However, most are easy-to-use techniques available to every employee to assist objective communication about our day-to-day work issues. The one common thread is that all encourage collaboration and teamwork between management and workers. They can be broadly categorised as falling under the following headings:

- Measurement
- Process management
- Problem solving and corrective action

These systems and tools are used to eliminate error and to reduce variation. Elements are used in association with a change in management behaviour to encourage innovation. We will consider the scope of many of these tools over the next few days.

From the planning perspective we need to be aware of the 'toolkit' available to assist us in the change process. We need to be aware of the traps that some have encountered in implementing TQM. There is a temptation to become obsessed with tools such as statistical process control as the only method needed for continuous improvement. A small, ad hoc group should be assigned to study all the tools available and advise on their applicability to our organisation.

Key opportunities

Our plan has to ensure that we tackle key business issues or problems whilst we are changing the business culture.

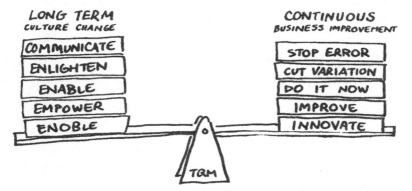

Our assessment highlighted a number of problems we encounter in our day-to-day operations and provided some indication or benchmark of what we have to achieve to gain a competitive advantage. We should view these areas as key opportunities for improvement. However, commonsense tells us that we cannot deal with every opportunity immediately; we need to set some priorities.

All these opportunities will be the result of something wrong in our work processes. For example, if we have found that our overdue receivables are causing cash flow problems we will need to analyse and improve the billing process. That is a large process made up of many small processes centred in several departments and involving a number of people.

The planning job is to select some key processes for early analysis and improvement. These will ensure that our investment brings an immediate return in business improvement.

Implementation tactics

Once approved, our plan will have to be implemented. We will need to create an awareness of the need to change and provide an environment for success. Everyone in the organisation will have a role in the process and will therefore have a right to know how and when. The tactics to achieve this awareness must be included in the plan.

To assist us in completing this element of the plan, we should consider the following questions:

1 Are we going to implement TQM across the whole organisation right from the start, or are we going to select some pilot divisions or locations?
2 Announcing our plans too early could create expectations that will be difficult to meet but announcing them too late could create confusion and rumour. When and what do we announce?
3 In our culture, what would be the most effective medium to ensure awareness?
4 How will we avoid or handle possible scepticism or even cynicism?
5 What other initiatives have been launched in the past, or are on-going, and how do they relate to TQM?

Remember, this is not a mere motivational exercise, so a good guideline is 'facts not hype'.

Goals and criteria for success

To ensure that we keep on course and that our plan is working, we need to establish short and long-term goals for our TQM process.

The assessment will have provided us with a base-line in both the cultural and business aspects of our organisation which we will now use to set progress markers for our journey. They should be both short-term (for example, quarterly) and long-term.

The progress markers will include the specific cultural change expected, the TQM plan deadlines and outputs, and specific business improvements.

Our plan will define all these progress markers, and will define the method and timing of reviews and audits of the process, as measuring and monitoring the progress of TQM is essential.

Resources required

Implementation of each element of our plan will require resources. This is a business plan, so they must be estimated and included in the plan. Success requires on-going management commitment so management need to know to what they are committed from the outset. Sudden surprises could easily bring the whole process to a grinding halt.

Resources could include payment for materials and outside consultants or suppliers. However, the largest element is most likely to be time. That is time to be taken away from normal work to implement TQM. Time for education at all levels, for meetings of specialist groups and for monitoring the process.

Summary

We have spent Tuesday considering all the elements involved in preparing an implementation plan for TQM. We looked at:

- Establishing a planning team
- Vision, principles and values
- Structure for change
- Education and training
- Systems and tools
- Goals and criteria
- Resources needed

In practice, a planning team would take several days to consider all these issues and then a period as individuals or small groups 'working up the details'. The completed plan will then require approval or amendment by the senior management team.

What did the planning process show us about TQM in our organisation?

- Will it be easy to implement?
- Who will be involved?
- How long will it take?
- How will we know if it is working?

Providing the environment

Executives and senior managers have the crucial role in the creation of an organisation committed to total and continuous improvement. No one else has the authority or control of resources to *make it happen*. It most certainly will not happen just by desire or by accident. Executives must plan for it to happen and then cause it to happen.

Making it happen can best be perceived as containing three elements. These elements can be summarised as changing the culture or providing the environment, providing the process and providing the support. Today we will concentrate on the first element, providing the environment and on Thursday and Friday we will consider the other two elements. However, we must remember that no one element stands on its own. We need to maintain all three elements in balance.

Barriers to communication

Current management practices inhibit the real involvement
of employees in the pursuit of quality. Some of them create
barriers to communication between each level of
management as well as between departmental peers at each
level. But perhaps the most important barrier is the
implementation gap between the intention of executives and
the wholehearted commitment of managers and employees.

To measure the extent to which these barriers exist in your
organisation, consider the behaviour pattern exhibited by
executives when the following questions are asked.
Do the executives

- make decisions with little knowledge of the
  implication on the systems or people who have to
  implement them?
- communicate their decisions effectively to those
  charged with implementation?
- work as individuals rather than as a team?
- do what they say?
- establish measurable criteria for other than short-
  term financial or people measurement?
- enthuse the organisation with leadership?

Managers
The behaviour pattern of executives will influence the
behaviour and attitudes of managers. The questions we
should ask managers in our organisation relate to their
reactions.

Do managers:

- feel stressed in meeting executive decisions?
- lack enthusiasm for change?
- fail to collaborate with their peers?
- fail to communicate effectively and inhibit communication up and down?
- fail to give clear instructions or to lead?

Employees

TQM has been described as changing the behaviour of management so that the attitudes of employees will change. Measuring employee attitudes can indicate how management is behaving.

Do employees feel:

- that they are left in the dark?
- that they are last in the pecking order?
- scepticism and mistrust of management?
- unheard and unappreciated?
- unable to release their potential?

Behaviour patterns

Behaviour patterns are based on perceptions or beliefs which are in themselves assumptions about what is true. The trouble with organisational behaviour is that perceptions quickly become facts, because people tend to act within the framework of their perceptions. If we are to bring down the barriers to communication we need to change these perceptions. To do this, we need to find new ways of managing, working and thinking.

Old perceptions
The old perceptions and beliefs are rooted in the history of organisational growth. To some extent traditional management practices served industry well for a long period but they are now being challenged by a series of social revolutions which are rendering them obsolete. The traditional approach has been called 'Taylorism'.

Frederick W Taylor developed the concept of mass production which was best symbolised by the management style of Henry Ford. The major elements of this style were command, control and compliance. Jobs were designed so that each worker had one highly repetitive task and jobs that required many skills were replaced by narrowly defined jobs in which supervisors made all the decisions. The worker didn't have to think; he just had to be controlled. This division between the 'thinkers' and the 'doers' has persisted to this day.

Vertical organisations
Another legacy of the control principle are the walls constructed between thinkers and doers and between departments. The vertical nature of the organisation is a

prominent feature. When problems exist between departments, the problem-solving approach is to tell the boss, who informs his or her boss. The reality of the horizontal flow of work processes is ignored and managers retain the sense of security from control.

New principles
These old principles of command, control and compliance are being challenged. Modern business is too complex to profitably separate the thinkers and the doers. The social revolution is attacking the principle of compliance without which control and command are unworkable. These traditional principles must be replaced by new principles based on teamwork, consensus and creativity.

New attitudes
Increasingly intelligent and ambitious managers and workers will demand a greater say in their business destinies and quality of life. This will not be stifled by corporate procedures rooted in traditional practices. The successful organisations of the future will be those who master all the implications of the rising expectations of men and women employees; the companies that allow them to release their full potential.

Practical principles and values

Everything that we have discussed today should make it clear that the development of a purpose statement and supporting principles and values is important. But they will not by themselves provide the environment for continuous improvement. Management will have to put the principles and values into practice. They will have to 'walk the talk'.

Cultural change must be related to the business goals of our organisation. These goals must represent the soft and hard issues of managerial strategy. These issues are complementary, not alternative options. That is the real heart of TQM. Only new principles that maximise human potential will provide the ultimate business goals. To consider the degree to which we have to change we must ask some more questions of our organisation.

Do our managers:

- encourage open and frank discussion of business problems?
- seek the opinion of those who are doing the job?
- explain their decisions to those who have to carry them out?
- recognise the contributions of all involved in the job?
- set *collaborative* goals to encourage teamwork?
- listen to, rather than talk at, their subordinates?

Purpose to performance

The diagram below shows the areas which managers must attend to if they are to put our new purpose and principles into action to achieve performance.

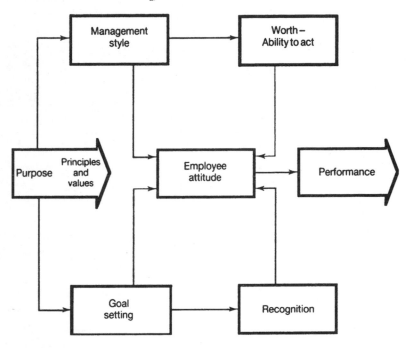

Executive role

Executives must take ownership of the new principles to the extent that they examine and amend all the traditional procedures and practices which determine employee attitudes. All too often, managers enthusiastically embrace the new principles which they have developed and then totally ignore the implications for their own behaviour. They must turn their attention to the four main areas described below if they are to provide the environment for continuous improvement.

Management style

The traditional style of control and command must be replaced by a participatory and listening style. A style based on leadership rather than management. The role of managers is to help people achieve improved performance rather than just order improvement. Seek their collaboration rather than insisting on blind compliance.

Worth

A confident and proud workforce will add a colossal value to the overall performance of an organisation. Employee confidence and self-esteem as part of a team leads to pride in their work and their company. Management recognition of the worth of employees as individuals is a determining factor in developing this attitude amongst employees.

Ability to act

Deep down, a sense of personal worth comes from the realisation that they as individuals can influence the organisation. The level of influence, in a sense demanded, will vary from one to another. The passive personalities will be delighted that from time to time their opinion is sought by leaders. Active personalities will want to be leaders. For them delight will come from the ability to act upon their own judgement. This is the issue of empowerment.

Empowerment

Management controls all the organisation's resources. Individual ability to act is most often related to the use of resources. Releasing the potential of the workforce does depend on management sharing some control of the resources and empowering employees. However, empowerment should be introduced in an evolutionary rather than a revolutionary manner. We cannot afford to replace control with 'wishy-washy' management.

Goal setting

Management in the traditional mould is obsessed with the numerate measurement of people. Management by objectives, individual payment by results, piece-work and appraisal systems only reinforce the fortress mentality and actively discourage collaboration between departments.

To find the answer in our own organisation we need to ask, to what extent:

- do our methods of reward and goal setting actively promote mutual trust and collaboration?
- are our goals and objectives established as part of a mutual and collaborative exercise between management and those for whom the goals are set?

Recognition

Management will demonstrate its recognition of individual contribution by its commitment to change traditional practices and procedures. However, it should also encourage a mutual respect between it and the whole workforce. Peer recognition is a powerful motivator which provides self-esteem and confidence. Corporate values use phrases such as, 'we will treat each other with dignity and respect'. It is a sad commentary on modern society that simple courtesy is no longer the norm. Where it exists in an organisation it is immediately obvious. The employees are all smiling and 'thank you' seems the most common phrase on the lips of management and people.

Summary

We have spent Wednesday considering the 'soft' or human considerations of the TQM process. We have seen that these issues have equal importance with the business and technical issues in implementing TQM.

In summary we considered the following:

- Executive role in making it happen
- Creating the cultural environment for success
- Barriers to communication
- Behaviour of managers
- Attitudes of employees
- Traditional management practices
- New principles and attitudes
- Putting principles into practice.

Providing the process

Our organisation can define where it wants to go but it also has to provide the TQM process or the vehicle which will carry everyone on the journey. Our executives have defined the purpose of the organisation and the new values which provide the environment for change. They will continue to have a major role, not least in providing the resources and a constancy of purpose in ensuring that the change is taking place. However, it is the role of operational managers to make it happen; to provide the process by which the change will be brought about and maintained.

The manager's role

The are two aspects to the manager's role in taking ownership of the actions needed to make change happen. One is a fundamental change in their own behaviour from their traditional command and control practices. We discussed these issues on Wednesday and will return to them on Friday. Today we need to discuss the other aspect of the manager's role, the one of developing the systematic elements of the TQM process. These will include the organisational structure, the systems and tools to assist people to achieve improvement and the education for everyone in the organisation.

Structure

The departmentalised attitudes and empire-building tendencies of operational management are often in evidence when planning for quality improvement. They can result in a bureaucratic organisation which takes ownership of quality improvement. Another fortress is created and quality is seen as a separate function rather than an integral part of normal business.

Quality and business operations are not divisible. Continuous improvement is the responsibility of everyone in the organisation, not a specialist or élite group. Quality must become simply the way we work.

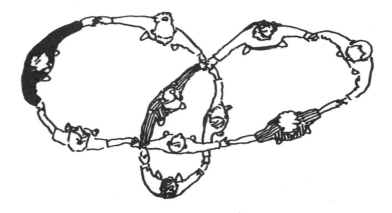

Tools and systems

In developing our plan we noted that we must make an initial choice of the tools must appropriate to our operations. This will form the basic toolkit which can be added to as the journey continues. Changes should be introduced at a pace that the organisation can digest. Each tool mastered and generally applied will prompt further development. The improvement process will learn from itself.

Competence in the use of the basic toolkit will form part of the TQM education and training. Other more sophisticated statistical tools will require additional specialist training. The task of the TQM teams is to ensure that charts, toolkit guides and other aids are readily available to all as they complete their training. The task of managers is to ensure that the tools are fully utilised by themselves and their own teams in the relevant situations.

Many of the tools and techniques used to support the TQM process have long been part of the management armoury or are derivatives of other traditional tools. For example, process mapping or process flow analysis are not dissimilar to established work study flow diagrams. Pareto diagrams and many of the measurement charts were in use as management aids in manufacturing long before TQM was conceived. We therefore need to consider the degree to which they are totally new methods within our organisation. How familiar are managers and employees with:

- measurement charts indicating error rates?
- error logging?
- corrective action systems to eliminate error?
- work process flow diagrams?
- run charts and process control charts?
- histograms and Pareto charts?
- establishing requirements?
- problem-solving techniques?

Measurement and analysis

What we cannot measure we cannot manage. This paraphrase of the teaching of Lord Kelvin is essential to an understanding of TQM. Many people fear measurement because traditionally it has been used to castigate them. But we all use measurement as a natural aid in our daily personal lives. Clocks, thermostats, speedometers and fuel gauges are all measurement devices. TQM seeks to create a culture in which measurement is seen as a similar aid in our daily work. To achieve this attitude we must concentrate on measuring the performance of our work processes rather than the people engaged in them.

Measurement can be taken too far; to use measurement charts as an alternative to wallpaper is a pointless exercise. Measurement and analysis must have a meaningful purpose. Both are tools used to communicate objectively about the performance of work processes and their use should lead to action. In the early stages of improvement (before managers have really learnt to empower people) this usually means communication between management and employees asking for help. Objective reporting and analysis of problems will free employees from the traditional 'shoot the messenger' reaction of managers to bad news. Management will readily accept the feedback from a control device, but not from a worker. Measured feedback helps to address this issue. Measurement becomes part of the common language of TQM.

Corrective action
The use of management and process analysis tools by workers and management will aid four-way communication about work. In other words communicating with peers in other groups, with managers and with subordinates. To ensure that management change their behaviour, listen to the feedback and then take action, a formal closed-loop corrective action system should be designed at the planning stage.

Many companies have elaborate error logging methods but rarely have a system to ensure that the root causes of these errors are identified and eradicated for ever. Too often workers are left to keep on 'quick fixing' the same errors.

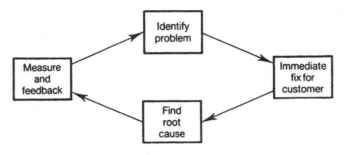

Problem solving
Identifying the root causes of problems is not always obvious or easy. A wide variety of problem solving techniques are available to help us with this identification. Many are already taught as a standard part of management training irrespective of any commitment to an organised quality initiative. TQM offers an organised process to ensure that their use is more widely understood and used. Most of the techniques represent a structured approach to the effective use of teamwork and brainstorming to resolve problems.

Control of processes
Many processes in both manufacturing and service organisations are designed and implemented to meet specific customer requirements, which, over a period of time, they are quite incapable of meeting. There is an almost automatic reaction, when the process does not meet requirements, that the people working the process are to blame. Usually the people are not the offenders. An

unaware management then provokes the whole costly divide between management and people that has permeated Western organisations. Statistical process control (SPC) is a powerful antidote to this environmental disease.

Reduction of variation
There is a variation in everything we do. We set tolerances in the standards we establish for the output of processes because of variation. In manufacturing, tolerances may be expressed in micro-elements of a centimetre or number of defects per million components produced. Service variation includes person-to-person, task-to-task and time-to-time tolerances.

All variation is caused so all variation can be reduced. SPC techniques can be used to measure variation and indicate its causes. Knowledge of variation theory is one of the most powerful tools a company can develop in its quest for quality.

Selecting the toolkit

The basic kit is unlikely to include the SPC tools which require more specialist training, but at the planning stage we should nominate a team to receive this specialist training. Their role in the TQM process will be to act as internal consultants to our operations, to select the processes on which to use these techniques. A manufacturing company will find more immediate applications than a service sector organisation.

Our selection will be determined by the need to ensure universal understanding of:

- processes
- measurement
- problem solving

Understanding processes

When we discussed the principles of TQM on Sunday we recognised the importance of maintaining the strength of every link in the chain of processes which provide ultimate customer satisfaction. This will be achieved by a thorough understanding of the elements of processes so that everyone involved recognises that they are a part of customer-supplier relationship. A powerful tool in that understanding is the use of the simple process diagram.

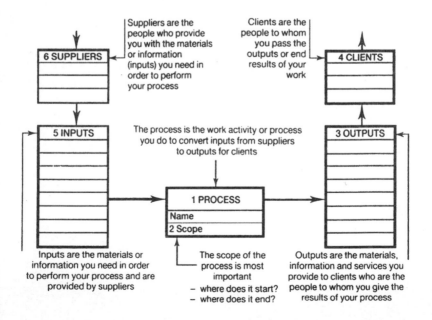

In practice, the process diagram must also define the management-provided resources which are constant to the process; the process requirements. These are the key to understanding that in the majority of cases, management or systematic issues cause more problems than the people working in the process. In the simple example below, only management can ensure that the right equipment is available, the procedures are defined and the people are fully trained. This is a very simple, or small-scope process, and many such processes are involved in a major process such as payroll or billing.

PROCESS DIAGRAM

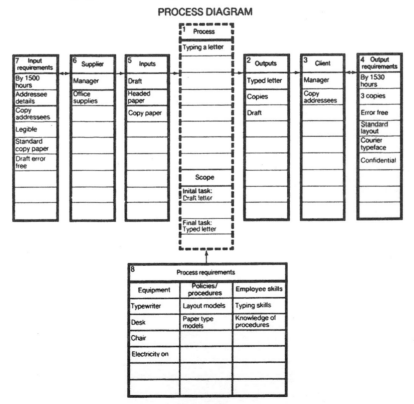

7 Input requirements	6 Supplier	5 Inputs	1 Process Typing a letter	2 Outputs	3 Client	4 Output requirements
By 1500 hours	Manager	Draft		Typed letter	Manager	By 1530 hours
Addressee details	Office supplies	Headed paper		Copies	Copy addressees	3 copies
Copy addressees		Copy paper		Draft		Error free
Legible						Standard layout
Standard copy paper						Courier typeface
Draft error free						Confidential
			Scope			
			Inital task: Craft letter			
			Final task: Typed letter			

8 Process requirements		
Equipment	Policies/ procedures	Employee skills
Typewriter	Layout models	Typing skills
Desk	Paper type models	Knowledge of procedures
Chair		
Electricity on		

Requirements

In a quality-led organisation it is the customer who sets the requirements. Management at all levels then has the overall responsibility for ensuring that customer requirements are clearly established and communicated. On a day-to-day basis, however, internal customers and suppliers of a process must discuss and agree the requirements between them.

In some cases, as in our example with the manager and secretary, people work closely together and so communication about requirements is simple. However, when more processes are involved, there may be a number of people who are working to the same requirements but who may not make regular contact with each other.

For example, the two processes of manufacturing a mirror and then fitting the frame can be broken down further into five discrete and successive processes as follows:

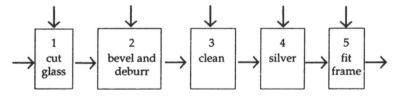

Process 1 which creates the size of mirror is a direct supplier to process 5, so those involved need to have a common requirement for the mirror size. All processes need to know the size requirement even if their process does not affect the size of the mirror.

We will need procedures, such as requirement forms to develop this discipline.

Measurement

Measurement quantifies situations and events.

Measurement converts subjective opinion into objective numerical assessment and is everywhere in our personal and professional lives.

Measurement in business has three major purposes:

- focus attention on requirements
- establish objectively the level of error in selected processes
- communicate clearly all the facts

Measurement is an essential element in the corrective action loop. The example below could describe the actions of a thermostat in a central heating system or equally the use of measurement by a work group in our own organisation.

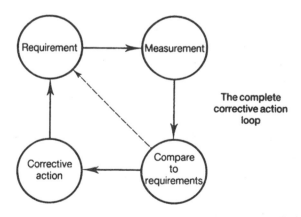

The complete corrective action loop

A typical measurement chart used to measure the incidence of error in a process is shown overleaf.

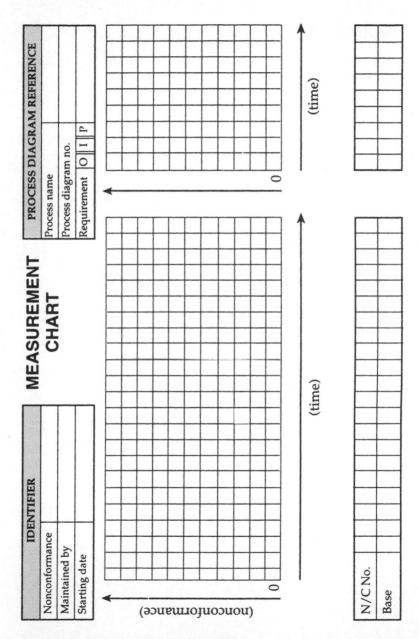

Problem solving

Problems need to be resolved. In many cases, this can be done between an individual involved in a process and a manager who controls resources. However, there is a complex series of work processes within our organisation. Solving problems therefore can often affect a wide group of people. The output of a team can usually be more creative than the sum total of individuals working separately. So the essence of solving problems is teamwork.

We have already looked at process diagrams and measurement which, as analysis tools, are powerful in problem solving. A typical group of additional problem-solving techniques which we may want to include in our toolkit are:

- brainstorming
- Pareto diagrams
- cause and effect diagrams
- critical examination matrix

The problem solving or corrective action teams will decide which techniques to use when identifying the root cause of problems.

Brainstorming
Brainstorming encourages creative thinking in groups. Team individuals throw up ideas which are recorded. All contributions are recorded and none are rejected. Each idea recorded has a tendency to fire off another thought pattern and idea from another individual. It can be used to generate

a large number of ideas about a problem in a short time. All the ideas written down are later evaluated by the team.

Pareto diagrams

Pareto diagrams are simply charts which identify and rank the major cause of a problem. Named after an Italian economist, Pareto diagrams are used to illustrate a common principle of distribution: most effects (roughly 80%) are accounted for by a few (about 20%) causes. For instance

- 80% of a doctor's time is taken up by 20% of patients
- 80% of wine is drunk by 20% of the population
- 80% of passengers are carried on 20% of the bus routes

Known as the '80/20 Rule', this can help a team rank the causes of a problem in order of priority.

Cause and effect diagrams

Cause and effect diagrams can be used to investigate each cause further and to distinguish between the main cause of a problem and its effects. There are two types:

- Work flow diagram, so called because it follows the main sequence of events, or processes, leading to a particular effect
- Fishbone diagram, so called because when completed is resembles the skeleton of a fish (sometimes called the Ishikawa diagram after its Japanese inventor)

The work flow diagram can be illustrated with the earlier process flow example for manufacturing a mirror. Possible causes of the problem can be identified and linked by arrows to the process to which they relate. This can be done randomly, considering the whole process at once in a brainstorming session, or sequentially, considering it one step at a time.

Work flow for manufacturing a mirror

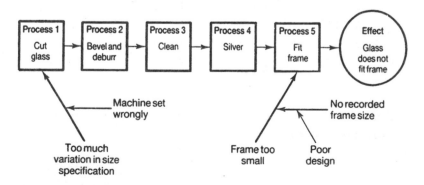

Fishbone diagrams are best presented on a large sheet of paper so that everyone can see and contribute as the diagram is constructed. Below is a typical approach.

Brainstorm each cause and write the ideas onto the diagram as shown in the example below.

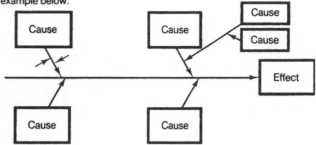

A completed Fishbone diagram for brainstorming the cause of a car's high petrol consumption looks something like this:

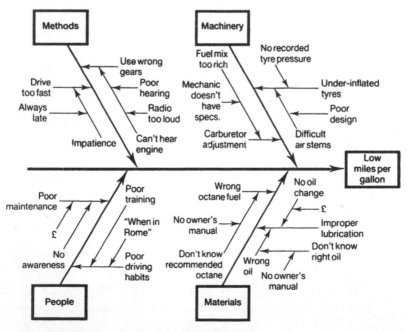

The critical examination matrix

A forbidding title for a simple and useful process which simply prompts us to answer questions about the problem. Once all the facts have been gathered, the team should analyse the problem and evaluate alternative solutions.

The key words, what, how, when, where and who, identify the purpose, means, sequence, place and person. Each of these factors are likely to feature in the solution. These questions can be tightly structured into a critical examination matrix like the example below. It is always best to use facts rather than opinions in developing a solution. Use the questions to prompt the team's thinking and the matrix as a checklist to ensure that nothing has been missed.

Critical examination matrix chart

present method	questions	alternatives	selections
what is achieved?	why is it necessary?	what else could be done?	what should be done?
how is it done?	why that way?	how else could it be done?	how should it be done?
when is it done?	why then?	when else could it be done?	when should it be done?
where is it done?	why there?	where else could it be done?	where should it be done?
who does it?	why them?	who else could do it?	who should do it?

There are a variety of other tools and techniques available to us to assist the process of problem solving and innovations. A pocket guide entitled *The Memory Jogger* published by Goal/QPC will provide valuable information.

Summary

We have spent Thursday considering what is required for the TQM process to transform our culture into one based on continuous improvement. In doing that we looked at:

- The manager's role in making it happen
- The structure we need
- The importance of a basic toolkit
- Measurement and analysis
- Corrective action
- Problem solving
- The control of processes
- Reduction of variation
- Some specific tools

Supporting the process

Intelligent managers, with their experience of business life, will have recognised the need to change. They will conceptually understand the reasons for providing the environment, in the sense of establishing a purpose, principles and values for the organisation. They will also understand the need to provide a process for change, in the sense of educating the employees and providing systems and tools for all to use. They may even understand the need to support the process of change, in the sense of changing their behaviour.

In essence this is what we have been working on since Sunday. Today we are going to delve deeper into the implementation of TQM and the issues that arise in supporting this process of change. We need to understand what has to happen if we are to involve fully our people and help them to release their potential.

Successfully implementing TQM is not easy. Aiming to be the best is never easy. Actually the principles of TQM are very simple and are in essence the application of sound common sense. Unfortunately, there is nothing so common in traditional management practices as the lack of common sense.

Despite being wedded to the new objectives, management have a tendency to fall back on the tried and proven methods of command and compliance. They try to control the implementation of TQM in the same old ways, though with courtesy and in the spirit of participation. Deep down, they have not really understood the level of change demanded of them to achieve a sustained competitive advantage.

TQM does require a profound level of change in the behaviour of management. They will not change the attitudes of employees without changing themselves. Both management and employees must change to unlock their combined potential for the ultimate success of the organisation.

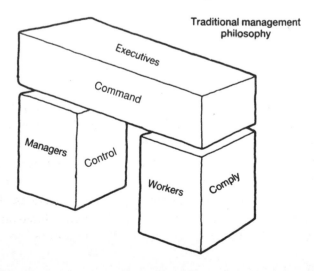

For the future, we must understand that education and the changing aspirations of people allied with the technological need for skilled people have destroyed compliance forever. The traditional division between the thinkers and the doers is over. We need to find a new structure that will be equally strong and will endure. The new approach will be based on collaboration and, as our diagram shows, it means a new role for the manager.

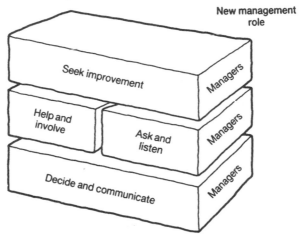

New management role

Consensus management

Consensus and participatory management are terms often used in conjunction with TQM. We must be careful what we mean by these terms. It does not mean decision making by committee or some sort of voting process. That could mean relying on the lowest common denominator. It is certainly not how Japanese management practises consensus. It has been said that for success, one should always have an odd number to make decisions and three is too many.

TQM is designed to ensure better decisions and collaboration in implementing decisions. It is not designed to remove the responsibility for policy or decision making from management. That is still the role of management and common sense dictates that it must be the basis of any organisation.

However, the TQM philosophy is about *how* management make their decisions. The barriers to communication that we have discussed all week result in too many decisions being made in a vacuum. Management do not gather some of the essential data for decision making. They must ask for the opinions of those who have to carry out the decisions. The people doing the job usually know more about it than anybody else. An executive policy decision to change the organisational culture to one based on continuous improvement is fine. The decisions about how it is to be implemented needs a different approach. Management need to seek rather than to order improvement if they are to successfully support the process of change.

Remember the Titanic
Many eager managers faced with the issues of implementation turn for a quick answer to the writings of the experts or gurus of quality. They take the statements they like from each and believe that they have the answer. This exercise has been called 'guru hopping'. But TQM is not a precisely defined methodology or a series of neatly tabled sequential steps or actions. Changing people's behaviour can never be that simple. At this stage it is useful to remember that the Titanic was designed and built by experts and the Ark by common sense amateurs.

Seeking improvement

Seeking improvement means asking for and listening to the view of those who will be most heavily involved in implementing improvement throughout the organisation. **Listening** rather than telling is the greatest change in management behaviour required by organisations who want to realise the potential of their employees.

Once managers have listened to the views and interpretations of those involved they are better placed to make the right implementation decisions. They are also likely to have a better understanding of attitudes and are thus better placed to remove the barriers to communication.

It is a mistake to believe that every employee wants to make decisions. But that does not mean that they are just not interested. An employee, whose opinion has been honestly sought and listened to, is much more likely to respond positively. If the reasons for the decisions are clearly explained the individuals will most often respond enthusiastically, even if the decision runs counter to their opinion. They have self-esteem because they have been recognised and treated with respect.

Helping people
In their new role, managers must learn to help people and ensure that they are fully involved in the implementation of improvement. This has been called empowerment of the people. In reality it is the empowerment of supervisors and first-line management.

Empowerment
Empowerment means giving supervisors the resources, time and support to become leaders rather than supervisors. Indeed the whole TQM process is about leadership rather than control or supervision. Allow them to challenge the way things are done and then provide them with the resources to realise their suggestions. Recognise their achievement and share their success. Build their self-esteem and ask for their help in solving problems. Encourage the new leaders to work closely with their people and a new environment of teamwork will produce astonishing results.

Role of the supervisor
Change can be seen as a threat to personal security and this attitude is likely to be rife with first-line managers. We have conditioned supervisors to control and controlling. For too long they have been 'piggy in the middle' trying to satisfy the conflicting demands of management. To leap now from theory to action could be a dangerous move. Before we can empower supervisors or trust them to throw away all the old, safe rule books, we must educate them in the new ways.

Train them to use the new tools of communication and leadership.

Changing management behaviour

Over the week we have discussed many elements involved in supporting the process through a change in management behaviour. The key changes required can be summarised as:

- Measure processes rather than people
- Eliminate divisive objectives
- Remove the barriers to communication
- Recognise that people want to do a good job
- Help people to do a good job
- Empower people to act
- Lead rather than command
- Listen rather than just talk
- Retain a constant purpose or vision
- Enjoy work and others will enjoy working with you.

Confident managers

We have seen that the role of the manager is to help the people achieve the task. The very best managers will also recognise that they need help from their people.

The most essential element in management development is to instill the belief that they are now managing; a belief that will provide an inner confidence of self-esteem so that they are prepared to be vulnerable. To understand that disagreement, openly expressed, from peers or subordinates is not necessarily a sign of disrespect.

To implement TQM, managers have to be confident. They have to realise that 'soft' or caring management does not mean weak management. Taking time over a decision is not a sign of weakness but the exercise of common sense. Seeking the views of subordinates before making decisions is the sign of a strong manager. A manager who seeks others' views, even strong disagreement, and then makes and explains the decision, will win respect and intense loyalty from the team. That confidence has created the team and given every member, at whatever level, their own self-esteem, their own pride. In this team everyone counts. Achieving that level of teamwork is leadership, not mere management.

Motivation

We saw earlier that motivation alone will not achieve cultural change but that is not to say that the motivation of people is not a part of TQM. Much of what is called motivation in business is the alternate application of the stick and the carrot; punishment or incentive. As Herzberg has shown us, this push me, pull me management approach may lead the individual to move but it does not motivate them. Real motivation is to give individuals a reason to move; the individual acts because they want to act. People motivated this way will want to succeed for their own sake but also for the sake of the manager, the organisation and perhaps most importantly, the customer. But before this level of response can be achieved the organisation must drive out fear.

Driving out fear
Fear is the insidious cancer which prevents organisations operating to their maximum effectiveness over the long term. It is created by the traditional behaviour of management but most managers do not recognise that fear is present. They would be horrified to believe that any of their own actions have contributed to a sense of fear amongst their subordinates.

Fear exists in the minds of managers and people. Typical fears found in most organisations are the fears of:

- Reprisal. the fear of being disciplined or even sacked. Fear of receiving poor appraisals or performance reviews.
- Failure. The fear of making a mistake or of making the wrong career move. Fear of taking any risk.
- Providing information. Managers and workers are reluctant to volunteer information which may be used against them.
- Knowing. Information is power and many managers fear that they do not know what is going on.
- Giving up control. Managers in this environment will select or promote people who they feel that they can control.
- Change. People feel more secure with what they know. This fear is the biggest impediment to the introduction of TQM.

Summary

Most of today we have been discussing the management behaviour and actions which are required to motivate people, drive out fear and provide a clear purpose. There are some further approaches and systems that will support the involvement of people. We will touch on those on Saturday.

Today we have considered:

- Success is not easy but it is common sense
- Profound management change needed
- Conflict between traditional and new management role
- Consensus management
- Seeking improvement
- Asking, listening and communicating
- Management confidence
- Motivation
- Driving out fear.

Before moving on to Saturday return to the list of concerns you developed earlier in the week. Consider whether they have been removed and whether you now have any new concerns about the implementation of TQM in your organisation.

Ensuring success

Yesterday we discussed how changing management behaviour could release the potential of people. Today we will consider some specific approaches that will help that process. We will then conclude with the elements of measurement and review of the process that will assist us to maintain a constancy of purpose so that we go on improving forever.

Wasted potential

In the traditional culture the most common method of seeking ideas is the company suggestion system. Most systems that rely on individuals submitting suggestions through a suggestion box or by memo are comparative failures. They fail for the same reasons that quality circles and other initiatives in that environment fail. Very little happens and there is little or no feedback. Management are not really interested and the people are not involved. This represents a terrible waste of the potential within our organisation.

The power of ideas

We saw on Sunday the incredible figures from Toyota, but they are not alone in ensuring success by using TQM principles to release the potential of their employees. Across Europe and the USA, organisations, both large and small, have achieved results way beyond their original expectations.

None of the successful organisations attribute their success to corporate suggestion schemes. Though the specific approach in each varied in relation to the size and nature of the organisation, the routes to success came from a combination of approaches which can be broadly summarised as follows:

- changed relationship between manager and employee
- process management
- improvement groups
- innovation groups

The first two approaches have been discussed earlier in the week, though they also play a part in the other two. Today we will therefore concentrate on the group or teamwork aspects of the power of ideas.

Improvement groups

The work-group education and training led by the supervisors of natural work groups leads to the first stage of real involvement. Initially these hour-long weekly meetings are used to encourage ownership of the need to change and then to provide competence in understanding processes, using measurement and problem solving.

These early education sessions tend to bond groups in effective teamwork, but the most important element of this process is that these meetings continue after the education and training aspects are completed. They are regular meetings of the supervisor and the team (of which they are now part) concentrating on improving their own process. They are now actively involved in a non-voluntary *improvement group*.

Guidelines for successful improvement groups

- natural follow-on to TQM work-group education
- specialist leadership training for supervisors
- initial concentration on small ideas to make group operations easier
- management support for implementing ideas

Key process groups

At the planning stage we selected some key processes to provide early opportunities for improvement. Early in the management education phase a key process group should be established. Their task is to analyse the operation of a major process (for example, the billing process). This will require measurement and analysis of all the sub-processes and the development of improvement goals or even 're-engineering' of the process. The selection of this team will depend on necessary knowledge. It will almost certainly

include the managers of departments involved in the
process and in most cases some workers involved in
process tasks.

Process ownership
When the group has completed its analysis and reported on
the improvement goals the group is disbanded. A manager
is then appointed to take ownership of the process with the
task of implementing the improvements. As the managers
of the departments involved have been part of the analysis
there should be little resistance to change.

Clearly the whole activity can be repeated for other
processes. It is worth noting that for every major process
tackled in this manner hundreds of small problems are
solved and the basic outcome of the process is improved.

Innovation groups

These are voluntary cross-departmental groups looking
beyond the elimination of error and attempting to innovate
and to find better ways of doing things. There is not the
slightest reason why these should be confined to groups of
workers and supervisors. They could be mixed, or operate
at different levels. This is a function of the organisation and
the sector in which it is engaged. Almost certainly these
groups need to be led by specifically trained group leaders.
As voluntary groups they may well meet outside official
working time and monetary reward could well be a factor
in their involvement.

Maintaining the impetus

Many face difficulty in maintaining the impetus of their
TQM initiatives after the initial enthusiasm has evaporated.
This week we have been addressing many of the root
causes for this disappointment so that we can ensure
continuous success for our organisation. However, there is
one more trap for the unwary that we must guard against.
This is sometimes referred to as the 'top down' or 'bottom
up' argument about the ideal approach to TQM. Let's
consider this issue in slightly different terms.

Culture/education driven
Some executives are quick to recognise that they are
unlikely to achieve sustained competitive advantage
without a change in their managerial culture. This requires a
substantial investment in time and money in educating
every employee but it is seen as a long-term global aim. As
the key is changing management behaviour, this process has
to start at the top and cascade down the organisation. The
danger is that this approach alone does take a long time to

reach 'operations' and provide real business improvement.
The same old quality problems that instigated the change
persist and so the impetus dies. Everyone is waiting around
for the culture change to be completed before tackling the
process problems.

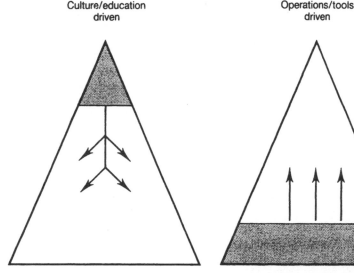

<table>
<tr><td align="center">Culture/education
driven</td><td align="center">Operations/tools
driven</td></tr>
</table>

• long-term, global aims
  management of quality
  suffers

• mixed messages
  quality of management
  suffers

Operations/tool driven

The alternate route to improvement, starting at the bottom,
also runs out of steam. The aim here is to train and involve
workers in the use of the TQM tools so that there is an
immediate improvement and a host of problems solved.
The workers want to do a good job so there is a high level
of initial success. Unfortunately, management has not
changed its behaviour and therefore the workers soon
become dispirited and cynical.

Results driven

Results driven

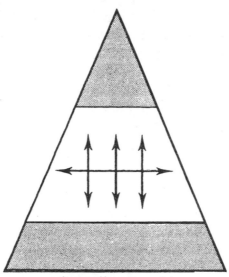

● short and long-term goals
  address cultural and
  operational improvement

We will ensure success if we address the cultural and
operational improvement aims as an integral part of our
improvement strategy. We cannot afford to wait around for
everyone to have completed their education before we start
tackling our operational problems. Equally, we are doomed
to failure if our approach is confined to the operational level.
The TQM process must therefore be driven by continually
achieving results against both short and long-term goals.

The ground rules for implementing a successful results
driven TQM initiative were established by our assessment
and planning sessions earlier in the week. We must now
consider how to use those ground rules to ensure that we
remain on course.

Measurables

The assessment stage of the TQM process provided data which effectively established base-line measures for the management of the process. The planning stage used this data to define some improvement goals and selected some priorities for action. The plan also recognised that TQM is a process in its own right and so defined some input and output measures for the continuous measurement and improvement of the operational management of the TQM process.

These activities led the executives to their initial commitment of resources to launch TQM. Planned improvements will help maintain executive focus and commitment. Executives are easily distracted by other issues once a decision has been made. They can also become very impatient for results. They will retain their interest and curb their impatience if they are provided with a continuous stream of relevant data that indicates progress.

Constancy of purpose

Executives expect to see success measured in business
terms. Such evidence will arouse their interest in the
cultural issues and lead to a greater comprehension of their
own role. The key areas therefore for maintaining
constancy of purpose from the executives are the business
measurables and the culture measures. These can be
summarises as follows:

Business measurables

- results of the key process teams
- improvement against the business improvement
  goals, for example, reduction in customer
  complaints, reduction in turnaround time, increased
  productivity, reduction in overdue receivables – as
  set in the plan.

Cultural measures

- evidence of increased teamwork
- more purposeful communication
- higher staff morale
- reduction in absenteeism and turnover

Process reviews and audits

To ensure that these measures are maintained and that
corrective action is taken where necessary, progress should
be regularly reviewed and reported. Process reviews can be
conducted by the facilitators on a regular basis and reported

to the steering committee. These reports should include specific measurement charts for each of the short and long-term goals established in the plan.

The executives should conduct, or commission, an independent audit of the TQM process against the business and cultural progress markers at least once a year. The results of this audit can be used as assessment data for the preparation of the succeeding year's plan for the continuation of the TQM process.

Enthusiasm

We have been concentrating on maintaining management constancy of purpose. However, everybody is involved and it is equally important that enthusiasm is maintained and enhanced at every level.

If management is steadily changing its behaviour, people will respond. But this will not happen instantly. It is important, therefore, that the people involved should see some purpose to their own efforts from an early stage. Recognition and evidence of success are the main drivers for internal motivation for supervisors and employees alike.

Success in this context will not necessarily be expressed in the same key measurables as presented to the executives. Remember that senior management is focused on the performance of overall large scale processes. Generally, the employees are involved in the small-scale processes that make up the whole. Therefore, success must be presented in dimensions with which they can identify and indeed emulate. Evidence that, at last, the 'insignificant many' are receiving attention will inspire others to join the cause. It will also show that it is possible for the individual to contribute and that effort will be recognised.

Summary

So, ensuring success depends on the organisation keeping score. At the highest level it will also be aided by a growing customer orientation. The organisation must look outward towards its market place, its competitive position and continuously update the benchmarks for success.

Today we have considered:

- Traditional suggestion system and the real potential
- Improvement, key process and innovation groups
- Top down or bottom up alternatives
- Results driven TQM
- Key measurables
- Reviewing and auditing progress
- Constancy of purpose and enthusiasm